T0193517

# It's Time to SELF-REGULATE
## WITHOUT BLAME

*Releasing Addictions and Strongholds*

## Dedorah S. Brown

WESTBOW
PRESS®
A DIVISION OF THOMAS NELSON
& ZONDERVAN

WestBow Press books may be ordered through booksellers or by contacting:

WestBow Press
A Division of Thomas Nelson & Zondervan
1663 Liberty Drive
Bloomington, IN 47403
www.westbowpress.com
844-714-3454

ISBN: 978-1-6642-9404-2 (sc)
ISBN: 978-1-6642-9405-9 (hc)
ISBN: 978-1-6642-9403-5 (e)

Library of Congress Control Number: 2023904099

Print information available on the last page.

WestBow Press rev. date: 04/13/2023

This book is dedicated to Mookie

Respect and gratitude to Vera, Granny, Ethel Mae, Ben Taylor,
Aunt Bert Tee, Papa JB, Cannon, Papa Collins,
Papa Clarence, Cleophous, Oscar, Russell, and Sonny Boy.

# Acknowledgments

Local female authors who supported my desire to write and publish books: Tracey Jackson, Suzette W. Rankins, Debra W. Gould, Jeannie Morin, Scarlett Miller, and Kemberley Washington, CPA.

Sisters who helped me pour into others with their kindhearted donations: Antoinette Hamilton, Destiny Martin, Gladys Clark, Judith Conner, Joana C. Platenburg, and Thais A. Sigur.

Sisters who encouraged me to seek God's word and be the blessing that I was designed to be: Dr. Kiki Baker Barnes, Tawanda M. Crayton, Angequela Ambrose Ambeau, La'Shonda G. Ambrose, Linda W. Lewis, Gwendolyn Smith and Tina Boquet.

Special recognition to Dew, Dank, Brittney A. Brown, Brandon J. Brown, Daff, Tierra, Sa'maya, Shawn Jr., Cannon Magee, and United States Veterans.

# *Introduction*

Some things in life are time-sensitive. Allow me to give you a few examples of time-sensitive matters, according to my New Orleans experience. If you do not eat your beignets immediately after they are prepared while they are nice and hot, they may be quite hard when you try to eat them later. If you are cooking a pot of red beans or a pot of gumbo and you (as we say down here) *don't watch cho pot,* you *will* ruin the whole meal. If you are watching the Bayou Classics football game and go to the restroom or go to get a snack during the halftime show, you will miss seeing something spectacular. Now this may be one of the most time-sensitive examples that I can share about down home, and please believe me it is serious business. The elders always advise one another to make sure that they take their blood pressure medications before watching a Saints football game because they are notorious for doing things that can have your emotions all over the place.

Some things in life are not time-sensitive, but based on one's stage of development at that time, they may have a certain belief system. Have you ever played the game hide-and-seek with children under the age of four? I have, and it is one of the cutest things that you could ever witness in life. At one stage, they may consider themselves hiding simply by standing against the wall with their hands over their eyes. At another stage, they may consider themselves hiding as they run and sit under a dining room table that has no covering; therefore, they can easily be seen. Not only can they easily be seen, but they can also be heard laughing. And if you yell out to them, "Are you under the table?" they may respond, "No." Sometimes they may be truthful and yell out, "Yes!"

Now this is when it really gets precious. The children are still under the age of four but are a little wiser now. They have played this game a time or two so now they are ready. Even if there are two or more hiding in the same space at the same time, they now have a different understanding of how the game is played. They now know that they must hide where there is proper covering so that they cannot be seen. They have also discovered that they should not respond to the seeker when asked where they are hiding, but this is when it really gets good. Since they now know that they need covering, they may hide behind a curtain, but they do not realize that the curtain moves when they move. It is clear that they do not realize that the seeker can still hear them giggling and possibly see all of their little toes wiggling with excitement from under the curtain. They also have not discovered that it is better that they separate and hide in individual locations.

Now this is when it gets better. Remember they are wiser now. They have more experience with this game and have put some thought into it. The seeker may yell out to them, "Where are you?" and utilizing the wisdom that has been gained from playing this game, the oldest child, believing they are whispering, tells the rest of them, "Don't say anything so that they won't know that we are behind the curtains, OK?" The rest of them who are utilizing their newfound wisdom and who also believes that they are whispering says, "OK!"

Classic hide-and-seek with little ones. There is no blame to be attached to the little ones for still not doing enough not to be seen or heard. They regulated their views according to their stage of development, and that is commendable.

Now this is a personal me, myself, and I example. I had an experience that caused me to change the way that I viewed things several times in a matter of seconds. I do not know how common this occurrence is, nor do I know if this is odd, but what I do know it that it was real for me and when I sat with it later in the day, there was no blame that I could attach to myself by saying I was confused, a scatterbrain, or anything else people say when your views shift, be it over seconds, minutes, or years. You are where you are until you adapt a more helpful view.

One day I was driving a few blocks away from my home and I crossed a four-way intersection. After I crossed, I realized that a police car was speeding up behind me with its blue lights flashing. This is where it psychologically goes down. I became concerned and confused because when I crossed the intersection, I had the green light, which meant I had the right of way. I thought, *I hope they are not coming after me.* But the police vehicle turned at the next corner. I felt relieved and said, Thank you, Lord!"

But then I realized that they were speeding in the direction of my nephew's school. I said, "Lord, don't let them be going to my baby's school." Then I thought, *But if something is going on at the school whereas the children, the staff, and the community may be in danger, let them get there in time before anyone gets hurt.* Then I thought, *But if that's where they are going, please let them have and properly use the skills that are needed to defuse the situation.*

I am telling you that my mind was popping like a bag of buttery popcorn in a microwave. I started thinking it would have been better if they were coming after me because I would hate if something bad was going on at my baby's school.

If that wasn't enough mind clicking, I thought about several unfortunate incidents that have gotten global coverage and attention over the past few years between police officers and citizens, so would I really want to interact with them? My mind demanded a response from me by saying, "Dedorah, you make that call: the school or you?" Immediately I said, "I hope that the officers are law-abiding, but even if they are not, and in an emotionally charged, love-filled stance, I'd rather that they come for me than go to the school."

Just like that, and just that quick, my views had changed multiple times. I was sincere about every thought that I had. Every reason that my mind presented was valid. Every feeling that I had was real, and everything that I considered included the views from my historical lens. At one time, I would have thought that I was straight tripping having all of those different ideas about one thing in a matter of minutes. I know better now, and there is no need for judgment or to cast any inadequate blame. There are simply times when we need to get a clear understanding of why we do what we do, say what we say, feel how we feel, believe what we believe, and respond how we respond. Then we must make necessary changes. It is time to get clear about our reasons without judgment and without blame.

Now let's get to this self-regulation thing!

# It's Time to
# SELF-REGULATE

# 1

*Do not get so interested in what others want from you.*

## Self-Regulation Note

_____

_____

_____

_____

_____

_____

_____

_____

_____

_____

# 2

*Whatever your stronghold is should not have control of you.*

*Self-Regulation Note*

_____

_____

_____

_____

_____

_____

_____

_____

_____

_____

# 3

*If what you are investing time in is
not in compliance with your quest,
consider which matters most.*

## Self-Regulation Note

_____

_____

_____

_____

_____

_____

_____

_____

_____

_____

_____

# 4

*When you are with the wrong people, they will do enough or say enough to let you know that you are with the wrong people.*

*Self-Regulation Note*

_____

_____

_____

_____

_____

_____

_____

_____

_____

# 5

*Everyone does not need to know about the dreams that you have stored in your heart or how you see them working out in your future.*

## Self-Regulation Note

_____

_____

_____

_____

_____

_____

_____

_____

_____

_____

# 6

*How much longer are you willing
to place your peace, well-being, and
life in someone else's hands?*

## Self-Regulation Note

_____

_____

_____

_____

_____

_____

_____

_____

_____

# 7

*Your current circumstance is just that: current!*

*Self-Regulation Note*

_____

_____

_____

_____

_____

_____

_____

_____

_____

_____

# 8

*Sometimes when you think that your joy was stolen, if you look a little closer, you will realize that you actually gave it away.*

*Self-Regulation Note*

_____

_____

_____

_____

_____

_____

_____

_____

_____

# 9

*There is no need to change your song just because you believe someone else sings it better. Sing your song!*

*Self-Regulation Note*

_____

_____

_____

_____

_____

_____

_____

_____

_____

_____

# 10

*When you betray your desires,*
*you betray your being.*

*Self-Regulation Note*

_____

_____

_____

_____

_____

_____

_____

_____

_____

_____

# 11

*It is important that you remember yourself
even when others forget about you.*

## Self-Regulation Note

_____

_____

_____

_____

_____

_____

_____

_____

_____

_____

# 12

*Your existence is to be shared
with others but not all of it.*

## Self-Regulation Note

_____

_____

_____

_____

_____

_____

_____

_____

_____

_____

# 13

*When people try to violate your space, shut it down!*

*Self-Regulation Note*

_____
_____
_____
_____
_____
_____
_____
_____
_____

# 14

*When you know better, you can say
no and be stone serious about it.*

*Self-Regulation Note*

_____

_____

_____

_____

_____

_____

_____

_____

_____

# 15

*Unify your younger self with your present self,
and embrace both of them as lovingly as needed.*

## Self-Regulation Note

_____

_____

_____

_____

_____

_____

_____

_____

_____

_____

# 16

---

*Self-discovery can come at any point of your life.*

## Self-Regulation Note

_____

_____

_____

_____

_____

_____

_____

_____

_____

_____

# 17

*When roll is called for the life that you have designed for yourself, proudly raise your hand and say, "Present!"*

*Self-Regulation Note*

_____

_____

_____

_____

_____

_____

_____

_____

_____

# 18

*Some of the people who contributed
to the tears that you shed can also
contribute to the story of your success.*

*Self-Regulation Note*

_____

_____

_____

_____

_____

_____

_____

_____

_____

_____

# 19

*Live according to how you want things to turn out for you instead of living according to your mood.*

*Self-Regulation Note*

_____

_____

_____

_____

_____

_____

_____

_____

_____

_____

# 20

*People may have written you off, but get your pen and write yourself in a better space.*

*Self-Regulation Note*

_____

_____

_____

_____

_____

_____

_____

_____

_____

# 21

*You may need to change what you had in mind if who you had in mind does not wish to participate. You cannot make anyone support you.*

## Self-Regulation Note

_____

_____

_____

_____

_____

_____

_____

_____

_____

# 22

*Do not allow yourself to be used because someone is bored or because who they prefer to be with is not available.*

*Self-Regulation Note*

_____

_____

_____

_____

_____

_____

_____

_____

_____

# 23

*The only direction that you
should be going is higher.*

*Self-Regulation Note*

_____

_____

_____

_____

_____

_____

_____

_____

_____

_____

# 24

*When things happen that you did not anticipate,*
*collect yourself and continue to thrive.*

*Self-Regulation Note*

_____

_____

_____

_____

_____

_____

_____

_____

_____

_____

# 25

*Do not wait too long for others to share space
with you because they may never come.*

*Self-Regulation Note*

_____

_____

_____

_____

_____

_____

_____

_____

_____

_____

_____

# 26

If you are not interested in being critiqued by many people, do not tell many people your intentions.

## Self-Regulation Note

_____

_____

_____

_____

_____

_____

_____

_____

_____

_____

_____

# 27

*Instead of faking yourself out,*
*show up for yourself.*

## Self-Regulation Note

_____
_____
_____
_____
_____
_____
_____
_____
_____
_____

# 28

*Work on what you want to work out.*

*Self-Regulation Note*

_____

_____

_____

_____

_____

_____

_____

_____

_____

_____

# 29

*Pay attention to who you were, who you want
to be identified as, and who you really are.*

*Self-Regulation Note*

_____

_____

_____

_____

_____

_____

_____

_____

_____

_____

# 30

*The way that you share space
with yourself matters.*

*Self-Regulation Note*

_____

_____

_____

_____

_____

_____

_____

_____

_____

# 31

---

*When it comes to your wellness, there are just some things that only you can take full responsibility for.*

*Self-Regulation Note*

_____

_____

_____

_____

_____

_____

_____

_____

_____

_____

# 32

*Sometimes things may seem so bad that you are afraid to want, desire, or go after anything, but you must.*

*Self-Regulation Note*

_____

_____

_____

_____

_____

_____

_____

_____

_____

# 33

*If you believe that the things you dreamed
of are worth going after, go for them.*

*Self-Regulation Note*

_____

_____

_____

_____

_____

_____

_____

_____

_____

_____

# 34

*There is nothing light about the feelings attached to being betrayed by someone who you thought would always have your back, but use it as a teaching moment instead of letting it stunt your growth.*

*Self-Regulation Note*

_____

_____

_____

_____

_____

_____

_____

_____

_____

# 35

*What you want is worth showing up for!*

*Self-Regulation Note*

_____

_____

_____

_____

_____

_____

_____

_____

_____

_____

# 36

*Focus less on what you should leave behind and what you are more than likely to lose when what you will gain will aid in your healing.*

## Self-Regulation Note

_____

_____

_____

_____

_____

_____

_____

_____

_____

# 37

*If you wish to heal from whatever your whatever is, get as many positive and self-motivating tools that you can and use them.*

*Self-Regulation Note*

_____

_____

_____

_____

_____

_____

_____

_____

_____

_____

# 38

*Risking some things to get to other things
doesn't have to be seen as bad.*

*Self-Regulation Note*

_____

_____

_____

_____

_____

_____

_____

_____

_____

_____

# 39

*Sometimes we incarcerate ourselves with locks, bars, and cuffs that do not exist.*

## Self-Regulation Note

_____

_____

_____

_____

_____

_____

_____

_____

_____

_____

# 40

*When we played games as children, we tried our best to win. Where did that drive go?*

*Self-Regulation Note*

_____

_____

_____

_____

_____

_____

_____

_____

_____

# 41

*This stage of participation should not pass by without your full participation.*

*Self-Regulation Note*

_____

_____

_____

_____

_____

_____

_____

_____

_____

_____

# 42

*You may get knocked around as you fight for your future, but at the end of the fight, the belt is yours.*

## Self-Regulation Note

_____

_____

_____

_____

_____

_____

_____

_____

_____

_____

# 43

*Sometimes the lack of support can hurt you more than the violation did, but neither of those things are enough to take you out.*

## Self-Regulation Note

_____

_____

_____

_____

_____

_____

_____

_____

_____

_____

# 44

*You have been broken a few times, but there is a place inside you that cannot be chipped, cracked, or dented, and it is that thing that will guide you through.*

## Self-Regulation Note

_____

_____

_____

_____

_____

_____

_____

_____

_____

_____

# 45

*Taking care of you is not just recommended. It's required.*

*Self-Regulation Note*

_____

_____

_____

_____

_____

_____

_____

_____

_____

_____

# 46

*Beware of those who try to take credit*
*for your growth and healing.*

*Self-Regulation Note*

_____

_____

_____

_____

_____

_____

_____

_____

_____

_____

# 47

*Your counselor will not know everything that you have gone through, but give them as much information as you can so that they will have at least some of the information needed to better assist you.*

*Self-Regulation Note*

_____

_____

_____

_____

_____

_____

_____

_____

_____

_____

# 48

*Go get what you deserve out of life.*

*Self-Regulation Note*

_____

_____

_____

_____

_____

_____

_____

_____

_____

_____

# 49

*During those days when you consider
giving in to your strongholds, remember
that self-sabotage is often avoidable.*

*Self-Regulation Note*

_____

_____

_____

_____

_____

_____

_____

_____

_____

_____

# 50

---

*It is one thing to see what you see when you look at others, but pay attention to what you see when you look at yourself.*

*Self-Regulation Note*

_____

_____

_____

_____

_____

_____

_____

_____

_____

# 51

Get where you want to be. Do not just imagine it.

## Self-Regulation Note

_____

_____

_____

_____

_____

_____

_____

_____

_____

_____

# 52

*Are you participating in behaviors that can be harmful to your body?*

*Self-Regulation Note*

_____

_____

_____

_____

_____

_____

_____

_____

_____

# 53

*Block all of the barriers that try
to block your mission.*

*Self-Regulation Note*

_____

_____

_____

_____

_____

_____

_____

_____

_____

_____

# 54

Create as many small wins as you
can, and in time, those small wins will
help you dominate larger ones.

*Self-Regulation Note*

_____

_____

_____

_____

_____

_____

_____

_____

_____

_____

# 55

---

*Are you your own personal bad habit?*

## Self-Regulation Note

_____

_____

_____

_____

_____

_____

_____

_____

_____

# 56

*Allow yourself to leave certain spaces available so that when the opportunity comes you can fill that space with something meaningful.*

*Self-Regulation Note*

_____

_____

_____

_____

_____

_____

_____

_____

_____

_____

# 57

*Some people are not supposed to
be in your circle forever.*

*Self-Regulation Note*

_____

_____

_____

_____

_____

_____

_____

_____

_____

_____

_____

# 58

*Those who may have contributed to you falling will be watching when you rise again.*

## Self-Regulation Note

_____

_____

_____

_____

_____

_____

_____

_____

_____

_____

# 59

If others see you as not being worthy, will you join them and also not see yourself as worthy?

## Self-Regulation Note

_____

_____

_____

_____

_____

_____

_____

_____

_____

_____

# 60

*You have been responsible enough to provide for the needs of others so you should be responsible enough to meet your own needs.*

## Self-Regulation Note

_____

_____

_____

_____

_____

_____

_____

_____

_____

# 61

*The more you go against the bad grain, true growth can come alive.*

## Self-Regulation Note

_____

_____

_____

_____

_____

_____

_____

_____

_____

_____

# 62

*Go all in as if you have never fallen
short a day in your life.*

*Self-Regulation Note*

_____

_____

_____

_____

_____

_____

_____

_____

_____

_____

# 63

*Your story should end as lavishly as you script it.*

*Self-Regulation Note*

_____

_____

_____

_____

_____

_____

_____

_____

_____

_____

# 64

*You must control the enemy inside of you
because if you don't, the inside enemy
will escort the outside enemy in.*

## Self-Regulation Note

_____

_____

_____

_____

_____

_____

_____

_____

_____

_____

# 65

*It is time to stop adjusting to what holds you back so that you can adjust to what guides you forward.*

*Self-Regulation Note*

_____

_____

_____

_____

_____

_____

_____

_____

_____

_____

# 66

*Come on and do your thing so that you can
get to the point where you can do your thing.*

## Self-Regulation Note

_____

_____

_____

_____

_____

_____

_____

_____

_____

_____

# 67

*You have spent so many years trying to claw your way out that it feels awkward trying to find your way into where you belong.*

Self-Regulation Note

_____

_____

_____

_____

_____

_____

_____

_____

_____

# 68

*Find your way to wellness and
wisdom without blame.*

## Self-Regulation Note

_____

_____

_____

_____

_____

_____

_____

_____

_____

_____

# 69

*Live your life through your own beautiful eyes.*

## Self-Regulation Note

_____
_____
_____
_____
_____
_____
_____
_____
_____
_____
_____

# 70

*Share with yourself all of the marvelous things that you know about yourself. Then you can use those reminders for your progression as you move closer to the marvelous things that you want to achieve.*

## Self-Regulation Note

_____

_____

_____

_____

_____

_____

_____

_____

_____

# 71

*Believe it or not, but the connection between your growth being tied to what once caused you despair is logical.*

*Self-Regulation Note*

_____

_____

_____

_____

_____

_____

_____

_____

_____

_____

# 72

*Working on your strongholds is necessary,
but working on your strengths and
aspirations is just as necessary.*

*Self-Regulation Note*

_____

_____

_____

_____

_____

_____

_____

_____

_____

_____

# 73

*Ignore those who speak against you.*

*Self-Regulation Note*

_____

_____

_____

_____

_____

_____

_____

_____

_____

_____

# 74

*Learning about how others made it through can be a useful tool, but find out what works for you.*

*Self-Regulation Note*

_____

_____

_____

_____

_____

_____

_____

_____

_____

# 75

*Encourage yourself, but also educate yourself.*

*Self-Regulation Note*

_____

_____

_____

_____

_____

_____

_____

_____

_____

# 76

Pay attention to yourself to see if
you are engaging in things that
are setting you up for failure.

*Self-Regulation Note*

_____
_____
_____
_____
_____
_____
_____
_____
_____
_____

# 77

*From time to time, check in with
yourself to see how you are and where
you are in your healing process.*

*Self-Regulation Note*

_____

_____

_____

_____

_____

_____

_____

_____

_____

# 78

*You cannot change your past experiences, but you can change the way you once allowed it to defeat you.*

*Self-Regulation Note*

_____

_____

_____

_____

_____

_____

_____

_____

_____

_____

# 79

Take ownership in the input that you want
to have on the outcome of your livelihood.

*Self-Regulation Note*

_____
_____
_____
_____
_____
_____
_____
_____
_____
_____

# 80

*You should know the truth about yourself because anything else can be considered a rumor.*

*Self-Regulation Note*

_____

_____

_____

_____

_____

_____

_____

_____

_____

_____

# 81

*It is one thing when someone does not keep their word to you, but when you do not keep your word to yourself, that is a different arena.*

*Self-Regulation Note*

_____

_____

_____

_____

_____

_____

_____

_____

_____

# 82

*Your peace should never be placed up for auction.*

*Self-Regulation Note*

_____

_____

_____

_____

_____

_____

_____

_____

_____

_____

# 83

*Refuse that part of yourself that tells you that your wellness is not yours to have.*

*Self-Regulation Note*

_____

_____

_____

_____

_____

_____

_____

_____

_____

_____

# 84

*When negativity is calling on you, remember positivity is calling on you at the same time and positivity has first dibs.*

*Self-Regulation Note*

_____

_____

_____

_____

_____

_____

_____

_____

_____

_____

# 85

*Things were not always bad, and things are not always bad.*

## Self-Regulation Note

_____

_____

_____

_____

_____

_____

_____

_____

_____

_____

# 86

*Create space in yourself for yourself.*

*Self-Regulation Note*

_____

_____

_____

_____

_____

_____

_____

_____

_____

_____

# 87

*Commend yourself for speaking positively
over yourself because if you did not, you
would not have made it this far.*

*Self-Regulation Note*

_____

_____

_____

_____

_____

_____

_____

_____

_____

# 88

*There is no time limit on grief, but at some point, you have to decide how much time you will allow it to maintain its strength.*

*Self-Regulation Note*

_____

_____

_____

_____

_____

_____

_____

_____

_____

_____

# 89

*Give yourself the chance that you deserve
for true happiness and wellness.*

*Self-Regulation Note*

_____

_____

_____

_____

_____

_____

_____

_____

_____

_____

# 90

Opportunity is your friend. It's that kind
of friend that says, "Let's go to the movies."
And when you say that you only have
enough to get in but not enough to purchase
a drink and snacks, opportunity says,
"Don't worry about that. I got chuuu!"

Self-Regulation Note

_____

_____

_____

_____

_____

_____

_____

_____

_____

# 91

*When you continuously try to force a relationship with someone who constantly rejects you or treats you poorly, it is time for an evaluation. The evaluation should be conducted by you on you so that you can get an understanding of why you stay connected to those aches and pains.*

*Self-Regulation Note*

_____

_____

_____

_____

_____

_____

_____

_____

_____

_____

# 92

*You may go through some things that may take some things out of you, but they cannot take everything out of you. Sort through what you know remains solid, retrieve what you want to keep, and restore it.*

*Self-Regulation Note*

_____

_____

_____

_____

_____

_____

_____

_____

_____

_____

# 93

*Stop acting like you are not aware of the greatness that you carry inside of you.*

*Self-Regulation Note*

_____

_____

_____

_____

_____

_____

_____

_____

_____

_____

# 94

*Spend more time focusing on what you
want versus what has happened.*

*Self-Regulation Note*

_____

_____

_____

_____

_____

_____

_____

_____

_____

_____

# 95

*You may not know why things happened the way that they did, but use them for your benefit.*

*Self-Regulation Note*

_____

_____

_____

_____

_____

_____

_____

_____

_____

# 96

*There may be times when you do not do as
well as you would like, but hang in there.*

## Self-Regulation Note

_____

_____

_____

_____

_____

_____

_____

_____

_____

# 97

Yes, there may have been many rough patches
in your life, but march on in spite of them.

## Self-Regulation Note

_____

_____

_____

_____

_____

_____

_____

_____

_____

_____

# 98

*You may be hesitant about going after your dreams because you are harboring emotional scars from the past. Who would not understand that? But you must go after your dreams or eventually you will be harboring the disappointment of not going after your dreams.*

*Self-Regulation Note*

_____
_____
_____
_____
_____
_____
_____
_____
_____
_____

# 99

*There are some things that you have gone through that you refuse to share with others and that is alright, but in your silence, rejoice making it through it.*

*Self-Regulation Note*

_____

_____

_____

_____

_____

_____

_____

_____

_____

# 100

*Unburden your heart from past
and present burdens.*

## Self-Regulation Note

_____

_____

_____

_____

_____

_____

_____

_____

_____

_____

_____

# 101

*Work on it while en route to it so*
*that you can reap from it.*

*Self-Regulation Note*

_____

_____

_____

_____

_____

_____

_____

_____

_____

_____

# 102

*Get far enough removed from your issues
and close to your wellness, and become
an example of hope for someone else.*

*Self-Regulation Note*

_____

_____

_____

_____

_____

_____

_____

_____

_____

# 103

*You need to know who you are so that you can know how to respond to your adversities.*

*Self-Regulation Note*

_____

_____

_____

_____

_____

_____

_____

_____

_____

_____

# 104

*Having the desire for wellness does not eliminate the process needed to becoming well.*

*Self-Regulation Note*

_____

_____

_____

_____

_____

_____

_____

_____

_____

_____

# 105

*It can be hard trusting in people and things when so many people and things did not work out the way that you expected.*

*Self-Regulation Note*

_____

_____

_____

_____

_____

_____

_____

_____

_____

# 106

*Condition yourself to expect and
receive the best outcome possible.*

*Self-Regulation Note*

_____

_____

_____

_____

_____

_____

_____

_____

_____

_____

# 107

*Never leave yourself unattended
when grief pays you a visit.*

*Self-Regulation Note*

_____
_____
_____
_____
_____
_____
_____
_____
_____
_____
_____

# 108

*Rebel against thoughts, feelings, and fears
that tell you that you cannot do any better.*

## Self-Regulation Note

_____

_____

_____

_____

_____

_____

_____

_____

_____

_____

# 109

*If things do not seem to be working out for you,*
*regroup and step out of your comfort zone.*

*Self-Regulation Note*

_____

_____

_____

_____

_____

_____

_____

_____

_____

_____

# 110

*Do not avoid the obligation needed
to become a better you.*

*Self-Regulation Note*

_____

_____

_____

_____

_____

_____

_____

_____

_____

_____

# 111

*Once you get to that place of wellness,
do not forget that little person inside of
you who inspired you to get there.*

## Self-Regulation Note

_____

_____

_____

_____

_____

_____

_____

_____

_____

_____

# 112

*Release the pain of things that disempower you.*

*Self-Regulation Note*

_____

_____

_____

_____

_____

_____

_____

_____

_____

_____

# 113

*Take all of the limiting beliefs that you have about yourself and your future and allow them to vanish into thin air.*

## Self-Regulation Note

_____

_____

_____

_____

_____

_____

_____

_____

_____

# 114

*Pain can be flipped into something inspirational.*

*Self-Regulation Note*

_____

_____

_____

_____

_____

_____

_____

_____

_____

_____

_____

# 115

*You may not like everything about yourself, but love yourself enough to change what you can.*

## Self-Regulation Note

_____

_____

_____

_____

_____

_____

_____

_____

_____

_____

# 116

*Grant yourself a wellness pardon
from the unjustified life sentence that
you were groomed to serve.*

*Self-Regulation Note*

_____

_____

_____

_____

_____

_____

_____

_____

_____

_____

# 117

*Release the paranoia of what your life once was.*

*Self-Regulation Note*

_____

_____

_____

_____

_____

_____

_____

_____

_____

_____

# 118

*Devote more time to becoming better so that you can become outstanding.*

*Self-Regulation Note*

_____

_____

_____

_____

_____

_____

_____

_____

_____

_____

# 119

*Do not be so cautious that you decide not to be.*

*Self-Regulation Note*

_____

_____

_____

_____

_____

_____

_____

_____

_____

_____

# 120

*Take control of your activities, and
take control of your habits.*

*Self-Regulation Note*

_____

_____

_____

_____

_____

_____

_____

_____

_____

_____

# 121

*You can learn from others without agreeing with all of their views.*

*Self-Regulation Note*

_____

_____

_____

_____

_____

_____

_____

_____

_____

# 122

*Learn to trust your abilities so that you do not have to rely so heavily on someone else's.*

## Self-Regulation Note

_____

_____

_____

_____

_____

_____

_____

_____

_____

# 123

*If you do not respect yourself, others
will join you on that adventure.*

*Self-Regulation Note*

_____

_____

_____

_____

_____

_____

_____

_____

_____

_____

# 124

*Do not reject your creativity.*

*Self-Regulation Note*

_____

_____

_____

_____

_____

_____

_____

_____

_____

_____

# 125

*If you do not like the way that you live,*
*then change the way that you live.*

## Self-Regulation Note

_____

_____

_____

_____

_____

_____

_____

_____

_____

_____

# 126

*You will never feel totally abandoned if you do not abandon yourself. Always have your own back.*

*Self-Regulation Note*

_____

_____

_____

_____

_____

_____

_____

_____

_____

_____

# 127

*Do not tolerate being mistreated, and do not expect others to allow you to mistreat them.*

*Self-Regulation Note*

_____

_____

_____

_____

_____

_____

_____

_____

_____

_____

# 128

*Some obstacles are not meant to stop you. Some may come to give you a chance to see things in a new light.*

*Self-Regulation Note*

_____

_____

_____

_____

_____

_____

_____

_____

_____

_____

# 129

*Your self-esteem will not come from that kinship that you want to embrace you.*

*Self-Regulation Note*

_____

_____

_____

_____

_____

_____

_____

_____

_____

_____

# 130

*Check in with yourself to see if you
are holding on to memories of things
that are not serving you well.*

*Self-Regulation Note*

_____

_____

_____

_____

_____

_____

_____

_____

_____

# 131

*When you know where your gifts should be utilized, take them there and use them there.*

*Self-Regulation Note*

_____

_____

_____

_____

_____

_____

_____

_____

_____

_____

# 132

*It is alright to battle your situations
and circumstances, but do not battle
the life that you long for.*

*Self-Regulation Note*

_____

_____

_____

_____

_____

_____

_____

_____

_____

_____

# 133

*Get back to full capacity, where you belong.*

*Self-Regulation Note*

_____

_____

_____

_____

_____

_____

_____

_____

_____

_____

# 134

*Why live and act like something that bothers you is not having a negative effect on you when clearly it is?*

*Self-Regulation Note*

_____

_____

_____

_____

_____

_____

_____

_____

_____

# 135

*The part of you that you struggle with
and the part of you that you ignore must
get the proper attention that it needs
before it self-destructs the rest of you.*

*Self-Regulation Note*

_____

_____

_____

_____

_____

_____

_____

_____

_____

_____

# 136

*Your inner strength is waiting for you
to say the word and it will show up.*

*Self-Regulation Note*

_____

_____

_____

_____

_____

_____

_____

_____

_____

_____

# 137

*It is not that you do not want to function in a certain way. It is just that you do not yet know how to function in a different way.*

## Self-Regulation Note

_____

_____

_____

_____

_____

_____

_____

_____

_____

# 138

*Your thoughts may try to play you, but when you knowingly and intentionally play yourself, that is something totally different.*

## Self-Regulation Note

---

---

---

---

---

---

---

---

---

# 139

*Your mind, your body, and your being will give you hints and clues that it is time to make some changes in the way that you think and how you conduct yourself.*

## Self-Regulation Note

_____

_____

_____

_____

_____

_____

_____

_____

_____

# 140

*Take your place in which you are
meant to be and flourish.*

## Self-Regulation Note

_____

_____

_____

_____

_____

_____

_____

_____

_____

_____

# 141

*There is a difference between needing to change your ways and wanting to change your ways.*

*Self-Regulation Note*

_____

_____

_____

_____

_____

_____

_____

_____

_____

_____

# 142

*There is a choice that will be made either for you*
*or by you, but you should choose if you can.*

*Self-Regulation Note*

_____

_____

_____

_____

_____

_____

_____

_____

_____

# 143

*Pay attention to your instincts and how you or if you use them.*

*Self-Regulation Note*

_____

_____

_____

_____

_____

_____

_____

_____

_____

_____

_____

# 144

*When less than genuine thoughts cross your heart and mind, remember to fight through them to recall what you know to be true.*

*Self-Regulation Note*

_____

_____

_____

_____

_____

_____

_____

_____

_____

# 145

*One day when you have finally been rescued, you will realize that you were your own superhero all along. Surprise!*

## Self-Regulation Note

_____

_____

_____

_____

_____

_____

_____

_____

_____

_____

_____

# 146

*You do not have to start from scratch to regroup.*

*Self-Regulation Note*

_____

_____

_____

_____

_____

_____

_____

_____

_____

_____

# 147

*There is no true peace when you choose
to maintain a life filled with turmoil.*

*Self-Regulation Note*

_____

_____

_____

_____

_____

_____

_____

_____

_____

# 148

*Your situation does not have to be different at
the time that you change your views about it.*

*Self-Regulation Note*

_____

_____

_____

_____

_____

_____

_____

_____

_____

# 149

*If it is time to change your situation,
consider changing some of the unhealthy
things that you engage in.*

*Self-Regulation Note*

_____

_____

_____

_____

_____

_____

_____

_____

_____

_____

# 150

*What you nurture can lead to your
demise or your recovery. Beware.*

*Self-Regulation Note*

_____

_____

_____

_____

_____

_____

_____

_____

_____

_____

# 151

*It takes a certain amount of endurance
to defeat and release addictions and
strongholds, but you have what it takes.*

*Continue marching on and be well!*

*Self-Regulation Note*

_____

_____

_____

_____

_____

_____

_____

_____

_____

_____

Printed in the United States
by Baker & Taylor Publisher Services